Your Life, Your Destiny, Your Choice

By J.A. Carlton

AF408791

Other Works By JA Carlton

Fiction

The Freedom Fighter trilogy:

Wednesday's Child

Into The Fire

Fortune's Tide

The Heroes of the Line Series:

Nick, of Time; Heroes of the Line Book 1

Second Hand; Heroes of the Line Book 2

The Third Race; Heroes of the Line Book 3

The Fourth Tier; Heroes of the Line Book 4

Broken

Soul Hunter

Non-Fiction

Touch Me, A Beginner's Guide to Massage

Follow at:

www.jacarlton.com

Facebook: www.facebook.com/jacarltonauthor/

Gratitude

There are far too many to thank for this book, but I'll start out with my mother.

Barbara Lee, Mom, I miss you.

Bob, Dad, I love you.

Jeff, I love you more than you'll ever know.

Pop, THANK YOU! And I will never stop missing you.

Gram, you had the patience of Job, I'm glad we had such good time together.

Jodi, just remember... you started this!

Laney, Kat, Carol, all my SPN Family!

Jared, Jensen, Krip, Kast and Krew

#Alwayskeepfighting

Introduction

Over the years I've learned that everything that 'happens' in our lives comes to us through choice, whether someone else's, or our own*. As children our lives are affected by the choices made by others, sometimes on *our* behalf, sometimes on *their* behalf, with the children involved little more than barely considered possible casualties or beneficiaries. (*In a more esoteric way these choices were ones that some scholars, theologians, and philosophers argue we are still responsible for, having made them before entering into this life.) The concept is moot, we're here, the choices have been made, we must deal with them and the consequences of them.

This book is about taking off the blinders and starting at the beginning by giving anyone who's ever felt powerless a reason to remember that no matter who's held it in the past, the destiny of each individual, and the shape of their future, is in their own hands.

Everyone has the right to find fulfillment, joy, peace, love and harmony and everything encompassed by these concepts. Most of us have been raised to believe that in order to have these things that someone else must be denied them. This is the second biggest lie of all time.

The 'ingredients' for what fulfills each individual, or brings them joy, peace, love and harmony is most likely as personal to them, as yours are to you. And even if some of these things are the same, the expression of them might be different, and because of that idea and the nuances involved, one of the first things you must realize is that there IS ENOUGH for everyone. It's true that 1% of the population holds as much or even more 'wealth' than the rest of the 99% here in America, but consider that even though that's true, there's STILL more than enough for everyone, why? Because not everyone has the same idea of what wealth is. That's the kind of nuance I'm talking about. For some it's being able to sit on a toilet seat of gold, but for most it's simply about having enough to be secure. THAT is a kind of wealth that we can ALL achieve.

Every choice we are presented with is a crossroad in its own right, some are larger and will have potentially HUGE impact on the course of our lives. Others are tiny but may have just as large an impact. The choices we make change our personal destiny, who we think we are, and who we allow ourselves to be. But we limit ourselves when we don't occasionally stop to check where we are, to check the intersection we're standing at and see if we're really headed in the direction we want to go. This is about stopping and using yourself and all the internal tools at your disposal to make the best, most positive choice at each opportunity. It's about learning how to listen to yourself, and learning how to use the tools inside us to create a destiny of each individual's choosing in accordance with energetic laws.

No matter who you are, and what choices you've made before, as long as you are alive, there will come more opportunities to become all that you've ever hoped you could be. All you have to do is know they'll come and when you're faced with these choices, instead of acting rashly, or under pressure from an external source as may have been the case in the past, allow yourself to *stop* and truly consider "The Good, The Bad, and The Indifferent" of each of your options. Whichever 'you' comes to be in the wake of your choice, the key element is for that choice to have been YOURS and yours ALONE.

Everyone comes to the crossroads in their own time and in their own way, but even if the knowledge of how to navigate it sits in the back of their brain, everyone has the right to know that destiny is a matter of choice.

A Brief History

"Who are *you* to spout about MY destiny? Or talk about MY choices?" you may wonder. Well in a nutshell, believe it or not I might've been there or at the very least, deeply contemplated going there. I've made plenty of the bad choices, I've taken some of the well-intentioned advice and tossed aside my own inner voice. I've drifted in seas of disassociated ennui and watched as sometimes those I loved tried to eject themselves from the world. And then I've battled with my disgust over their lack of foresight even as my own floundered under the weight of years of disappointment.

For good, bad or indifferent I did what was expected of me. I was expected to skid by in school, so I did. I was expected to not go to college, so I didn't. I was expected to be the lazy one so I was. I was however, also expected to be smart and accumulate knowledge, so I did. I fulfilled the expectations that others had for me, (some would say projected onto me), and somewhere along the way unlearned how to be the person my childhood self, envisioned in the future. Well I'm on my way back to that vision, keeping what works, tossing what doesn't and doing my best to make better choices to get back to that positive vision.

It's taken a lifetime to get just this far, but the journey's barely begun. Everything up to this point, has been in a way, hitting the local bazaar for supplies. Whatever equipment I don't have yet that I'll need, I'll pick up along the way, I'm sure of that now.

So walk with me to the crossroads and see if any of the tools I have can help you on your own journey.

(Told you it was brief).

The Hierarchies

In 1943 Abraham Maslow developed a Hierarchy of Human Needs. By studying some of the most successful people of both history and his own time, he developed the following graph with the understanding that the higher levels cannot be reached without the needs of the lower ones being met. However in many cases, somewhere along the line, often just above the basic physiologic needs (the lowest tier) we get partially stuck in the next level; so that even as we reach for the higher tiers there's always part of us that just doesn't seem to be able to completely move onward and upward.

Fig. 1 is Maslow's hierarchy as it was conceived to represent the ideally average individual.

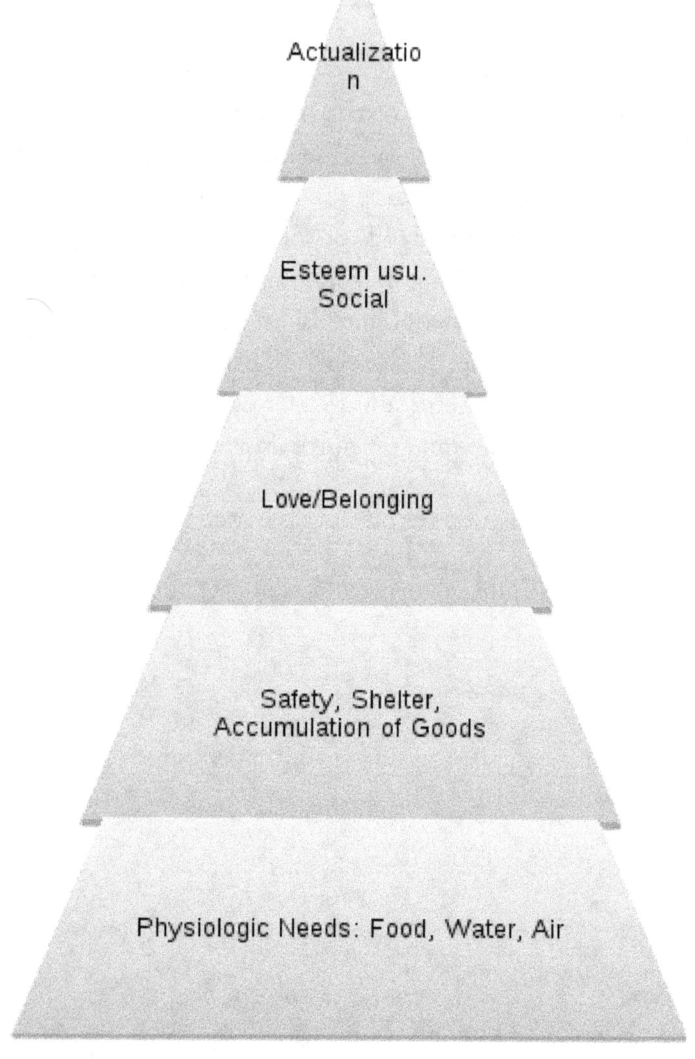

Maslow's Hierarchy – unrestricted. Fig. 1 (Wall #1)

In the cases of individuals raised or living in an abusive or manipulative situation, the following pyramid, Fig. 2, is a more accurate representation of these needs.

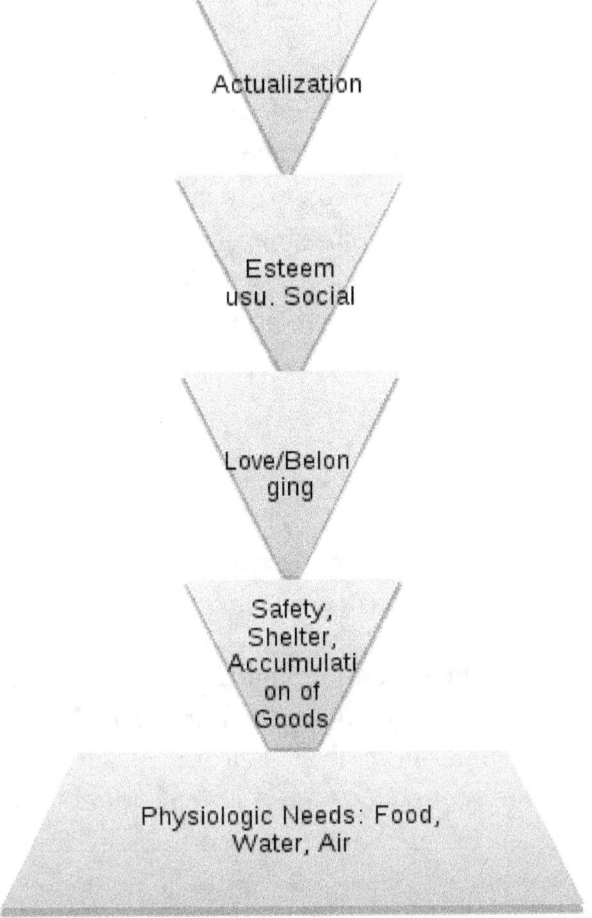

Maslow's basic hierarchy of human needs with restrictions.
– Fig. 2

When abuse has been the rule both of the bottom tiers have
been compromised restricting access to 'higher level' needs
such as love, (preferably unconditional) and belonging;
esteem, both self and social; and the concept of
self-actualization, or the ability to attain the highest level of

'self' possible, is an idea so lofty that it is frequently beyond contemplation.

In an ideally supportive household, each tier is solid, strong, and complete in and of itself, allowing for the individual to build their lives upwards experiencing each of these necessities in as stable a condition as possible. But in an abusive environment there is no stability. Each tier is in a constant state of imbalance precariously situated and ready to topple at the will of the abuser, which in effect keeps his or her victims under control.

The three middle tiers of Maslow's pyramid: Safety; Love and Belonging; and Esteem are what have been termed 'deficiency needs'. The principle being that without them, individuals experience anxiety and increased tension.

Whether it is subconscious or conscious manipulation, an abuser will keep his or her victims working so hard to obtain or secure these three needs from their abuser, that achieving anything more is virtually impossible, unless and until the victim/subject is able to extricate themselves from the situation and begin to repair the damage done.

This hierarchy was built to represent energetic, or some would call them more spiritual needs of the individual. Spirituality in this case is not to be confused with religion. Religion and Faith in whatever form they take, have, from the dawn of humanity, enabled individuals to summon all kinds of strengths they otherwise would not have believed they possess. These energetic principles are meant to show individuals that the power of their own destiny comes from WITHIN, from CHOICES they make on a daily basis.

Pyramid Wall #2 Energetic Hierarchy – The Foundations for a Positive Destiny. Fig- 3.

The following pyramid represents Community and its role in the life of the individual. Constructive socialization can be particularly useful for individuals who have suffered isolation either from friends or family, a tactic frequently used in order to exert more complete control over those who may pose a threat to an abusers self-proclaimed station.

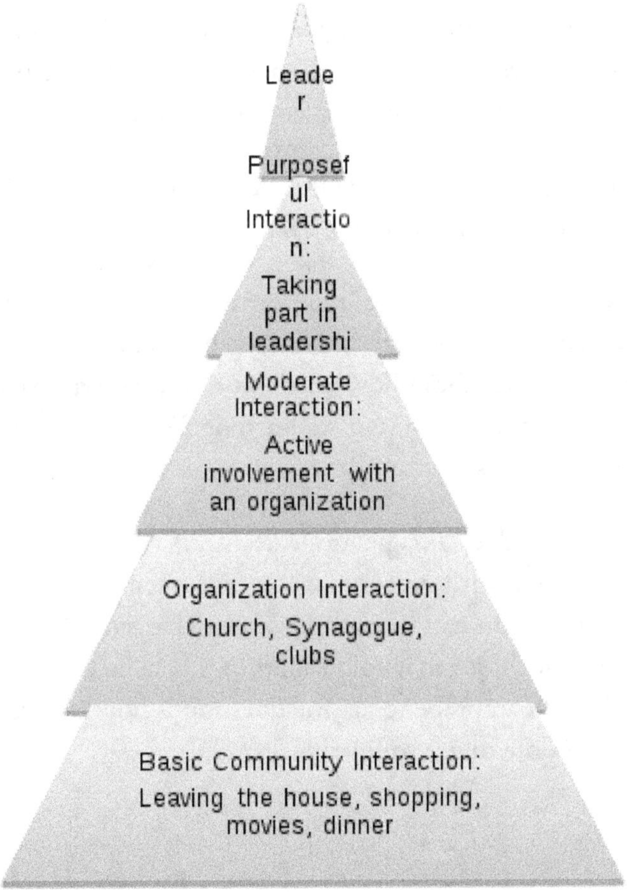

Pyramid Wall #3 Community Support. Fig. – 4

The fourth wall, the one that actually gives the pyramid its stability, the one without which the others would be far less stable or able to perform their functions should represent intellect and imagination both. The two are not mutually exclusive. Albert Einstein said, "Imagination is more important than knowledge". It was imagination that led him to his famous theory. It was imagination first that allowed DaVinci to conceive (visualize) of both his machines and artistic works. Without imagination the Wright Brothers may never have flown. Cell phones might not have been invented or computers, and art would be non-existent.

It's a fairly inarguable fact that it is the creative mind that has enabled our species to come this far.

It's also fairly inarguable that creativity and its mate, curiosity, breed knowledge and comprehension. If we didn't have the curiosity about how things work, we would have no desire to explore, which leads to learning. Without learning we would not exist.

BUT, knowledge, imagination, learning, curiosity, and comprehension without compassion, without grace are pale. Even imagination can be flat, devoid of character. It is the willful use of choice that colors all things imagined, known, learned, and comprehended. The question is how are YOU going to choose to use your will?

Pyramid Wall #4 Intellect/Imagination. Fig. – 5.

These four walls, ladders, levels of attainment, whatever you want to call them provide the greatest stability for any individual to build a positive future for themselves and those they hold dear, now, and in the life they choose to create.

When Choice Becomes Destiny

Having taken in all the previous information about the hierarchies and how they relate to both your well-being and some of the obstacles you'll have to overcome, now is the time to finally ask the question, "When does choice become destiny?"

The answer is, "It starts to, the very same minute you *believe* in it."

But here's *one* catch (and there are a few), destiny, and the choices you make on its behalf, is like a plant, it requires nurturing. If you think you're going to believe your way to president of XYZ Corporation and then not nurture the way to get there, shocker this, it won't happen. Lemme guess, that's the story of your life right? It was the story of mine, at least until I started truly contemplating and comprehending the meanings behind certain sayings and colloquialisms, and started to pay attention to the world around me. Once that happened I started to notice things, and once I started to notice things that were pertinent to my goal, more things came out of the woodwork to be noticed. Funny how it works like that, but that IS how it works.

What follows in the "why" is a combination of science, philosophy and insight that came from the culmination of experiences thus far. The information contained in these pages will always be in these pages so for now, based on who you are in this moment, and who you are yet to become; understand, practice and incorporate what you can and when you're ready, the rest will come. After all, it's already here.

Universal Laws

Before we get into either of the laws that will be used here, there's one thing you must find a way to believe, before you can believe in anything else; in your own power, or in your own ability to create your destiny. Before you can believe that you CAN build a positive world for yourself and those whose lives you'll touch, you have to believe to the point that you KNOW, whatever you've survived can help you build a better future.

There are some philosophers who will tell you that you CHOSE this life, and the things you were going to suffer, BEFORE you were born into it. You'll hear it. Whether you believe it, is a matter of your personal choice. What I believe doesn't matter, what anyone else believes about this subject is irrelevant. What matters, and the only opinion that counts here is YOURS. IF you choose to believe this or disbelieve this concept, it doesn't make you better or worse, stronger or weaker, it doesn't make you more or less evolved. It's just an idea, use it or don't depending on whether or not it fits into who you are on your way to becoming.

Once you know this, and believe this fact, you will have excavated much of your guilt and self-recriminations and can begin to lay the foundations of a positive future.

What are universal laws? They're rules that govern the interaction of energies in the universe, we're going to utilize the two most important ones in this book.

The Law of Self Responsibility

In childhood a great many of the things we endure are brought to us by various authority figures; parents, family, friends, and peers. These events are almost never the fault of the child. Our responsibility for the events in our lives begins in the early years of adolescence and ends when we're six feet under. The law of self-responsibility comes into effect as soon as you are able to know better, and holds true with even more certainty once you have become what society considers a legal adult. At that point, the consequences of your actions ARE your responsibility.

It's listed as the fourth tier up on the Energetic pyramid because it's something many of us struggle with on a daily basis. To get to the point where it becomes your nature will take a lot of work and probably facing up to a lot of things you might not want or be ready to see. Like all the personal stages, they're ALL points-in-progress, just like we are all works-in-progress.

This law is actually the most fundamental in that it helps the individual build their own supply of internal power. It's that internal power that helps provide strength when you begin using the first part of tip #1. Own your past. It also gives the individual strength when it comes time to forgive past transgressions that others have made on you.

It's the first step to honestly claiming or creating the life that's right for you. Each of us has to be able to acknowledge our actions and how they affect those around us. This consists of responsibility for all the intentional acts for either good or bad that we have each done. Power doesn't come from ignoring these things, it comes from acknowledging our faults to ourselves if no one else, and, (here's another key point), *acting intentionally to do better in the future.*

A 'Right Life' isn't about being perfect, my grandma used to say, "The only perfect people are Dead people." A Right Life is about doing YOUR best to make the most positive choices you can when you are presented with the option to make them.

Honoring this law is what lets you look yourself in the eye and accept that from this moment forward you will move into your future with integrity and sincerity. Once you make THAT choice, you'll find that so many of the others will come just a little more easily.

You Have The Power

What is power you might ask? Power is the capacity to perform effectively. In physics it's "The ability to do work."

There are those who 'wield' power out there in the world, those who can literally *command* the life or death of another human being, but the greatest power a person can have is power over their *self*.

Think about this, what would you as a person, think about someone who was able to rise above those who held power over others? Are *they* not more powerful than those who keep others 'in line' either physically/socially/economically or politically by force and fear? I say they are. And I am not the only one.

I do say however that the power that I am talking about is inside *you*. It is inside each individual to claim, to use or abuse as they see fit. The sword cares nothing for he who forged it, it's cleave is as indiscriminate to its smith as it is to the enemy against whom it's wielded.

I'm here, this book is here, to explain why you should *Choose to USE* that power rather than ABUSE it.

Gratitude

"Grateful for what I have, but always willing to have more." – Anonymous.

True gratitude is more than just being able to acknowledge the good things you have. Far too many people have spent far too much time simply listing all the wonderful things they have in an effort to find richness in their lives by learning the art of gratitude. True gratitude comes with taking the time to contemplate how you have attained those things that you have, as well as measuring what you've done to get them against the ethics of the person you want to be.

To some, gratitude is thanking god for the food on their plate even though it was actually their mother or father went to work and earned the money to purchase the food, then brought it home so it could be cooked and shared. They don't think about the people who makes pennies a day, doing back breaking work, tossing melons down the line, constantly in fear of losing their job and then subsequently having to wonder where their family will get THEIR food. They don't think about the people who run the farms that are frequently under so much pressure to produce bigger, sweeter, juicier, foods faster and at a lower cost so that the corporations who decide whether to buy their fruits/foods can make bigger profits while cutting the share that the actual farmer and his family make.

To some, gratitude is finding a quarter on the ground that will enable them to take a bus home on a sub-zero night so that they don't have to walk a dozen blocks in bone chilling cold and risk not being able to go to work the next day because they got a chill.

To some, gratitude is for the people who helped a terrified parent find a missing child, safe and sound at a friend's house.

Sometimes it's being grateful there's a warm blanket over you on a cold night.

Sometimes it's the passerby who hands off a bus transfer that has a couple rides left on it.

Sometimes it's the person who drops a few coins or even some paper money into an open guitar case on the street where a modern day minstrel is performing.

Sometimes it's something as basic as the ability to take a breath without feeling like you're drowning.

The point is to look at those things you have, a roof over your head that doesn't leak, (at least not all the time), food in your pantry even if it's just rice and beans, clothes on your children, and think about where these things came from. Not just your hard work that put them there, but what qualities you have that enabled you to achieve at least this much, and keep you striving to achieve even more.

And more importantly, it's to look at all the people around you, the store owners, the construction workers, the employer, the co-workers, the spouses, the in-laws, the older kids, the clients, who make YOUR life possible.

You Have Been Programmed

We have all been programmed by the world and people around us. We are a product of a program, that was a copy of a copy of a copy, (back into perpetuity), of a copy, of a copy of a program. Along the way there have been updates, usually controlled by some external, i.e. political, social, economic, religious, force. But, not a single one of us has written a completely new and personal program in eons. Fact is that most of us didn't even know we had that option. Well, we do.

The first step in making any change is the realization that change is possible. If you dare to embrace the idea that personal change is possible you will find yourself blocked, sabotaged and discouraged at almost every turn. Your desire to re-write your own programming must be stronger than any argument against it, even when the most powerful of those arguments come from within the program you're already running.

Before you read any further, there are at least 3 things you must know in order to make the best possible decision about the person you will become, they are: Homeostasis, Knowns and Unknowns.

The first thing you must understand is the idea of homeostasis. This is typically a term used in medicine. It is literally maintaining your body's 'status quo'. Keeping your respiration at a comfortable rate, your heart beat at a steady pace, your body temperature at a safe constant. But, there is both a subconscious and conscious homeostasis as well.

88% of our daily lives are moved through without conscious thought. We get up, shower, make coffee, eat breakfast, dress, and go to work, perform our job, return home, eat dinner, watch tv, check email, and go to bed, all largely on "Auto-pilot", neither fully aware or conscious of what we're doing or sometimes even why.

Subconscious homeostasis is a product of those automatic behaviors we do every day.

For example, you're on your way home when your best friend calls or texts saying, "Happy Hour! Meet us." At that point you are faced with a conscious decision that likely brings you back to the moment, weighing the joy and stress relief of happy hour with friends vs. the early night's sleep you were going to get in order to feel more refreshed for that big meeting or presentation tomorrow.

It is very likely that if you have a history of joining your friends for happy hour, that you will do so again. The choice is really not even a choice. What you will likely experience is a subconscious homeostatic drive to go join your friends. You know you will over-indulge, you won't sleep well and you'll feel like crap tomorrow as you move through your presentation or meeting, just like you've done an untold number of times before. You do this because the consequences of happy hour on the eve of a big presentation or weekly meeting are what's considered, in your life, a 'known'.

In all likelihood it's been so long since you've actually managed to get home and go to bed early that you are no longer sure if you can function optimally without the 'ritual' of a prior night's 'happy hour'. You tell yourself that if you went home and got to bed early that you'd most likely just toss and turn, wondering how the presentation or meeting will go. That in fact, you'll lose sleep because you didn't take the necessary step of having one or two too many cocktails that ensures you're out like a light as soon as your head hits the pillow. You have now not only enabled your own subconscious homeostatic conditioning, but reinforced it as well, by consciously justifying a negative-effect 'known' instead of making a conscious choice to face what has become an 'unknown', in the form of an early night of solid, chemical free rest.

Let's take this a step further and imagine that the meeting or presentation is not just another weekly hoop to jump through, but this time a promotion hangs in the balance. That promotion means an extra ten thousand dollars a year, pushing you from 40k to 50k a year which means you can afford to put that addition onto the house, which will increase its resale value by at least 10 to 15 thousand, AND you can afford to lease that new car too! That extra ten thousand a year puts you into a whole new tax bracket and headed toward financial security your parents never dreamed of! It's more money than you ever thought it possible for you to make!

So you make your fuzzy headed presentation, or you miss a few key points in the meeting, and you blame it on the hangover fogging your mind. Across the table a junior staffer brings up solutions to your missed points and gets the raise and promotion you've been angling for since you started in the mail room! It's NOT FAIR! But, it IS your program.

This isn't an example of flawed human behavior, this is an example of your programming, (headed toward financial security your parents never dreamed of! It's more money than you ever thought it possible for you to make!) working perfectly.

So let's run a diagnostic on your program.

You're 45 years old. You were an elementary school age child in the 1970's. You remember when candy bars were $.25 and giant pretzel sticks were $.02 cents at the local store. You remember penny candy, and you know that you were what was called upper-middle class because your dad made GOOD money, probably about $18,000.00 per year. Perhaps you recall thinking or hearing someone say, (or more likely you DON'T recall it) that making $40k a year would mean you were RICH, and easily firmly UPPER CLASS. And maybe when it came to those mysterious 'millionaires' you might have been told something like, 'we're not THAT kind of people' or 'don't get too big for your britches' or 'that kind of money changes people.' Each of the above statements carrying a negative connotation that people with too much wealth were not to be trusted, or thought they were BETTER than the 'little people' or 'average folk'.

All of the above sentiments came from an external source, probably a parent or other role model. It became a program, the inference being that you could make up to $40k per year and still be considered 'normal' and therefore acceptable.

So through this program, the number $40K slid through what we call a 'filter' in your mind, and into your subconscious mind, it became your 'Wealth Set Point'. Reaching that set point turned on 'homeostasis', and that point, that number, is where your subconscious mind will do everything it can to keep you, including sabotaging every effort to surpass that set point by keeping your subconscious focused on the results of behaviors whose outcomes are KNOWN even if they are deleterious to your eventual prosperity. The subconscious mind doesn't care or know about cost of living increases, it doesn't care or know about inflation, it doesn't care or know about the 'value of a dollar'. It only knows it MUST keep you at your 'Set Point'.

When the day comes that the average minimum wage is equal to $40k per year, your subconscious won't care. You may barely be able to afford a 750 square foot, one bedroom apartment but no matter what you do, you won't be able to break out of that $40k per year income bracket, unless your program gets rewritten.

Now let's take a look at the Junior Staffer's program.

JS was raised in an upper class setting, taught investing during the Clinton years where his modest savings spiraled into a high five figure nest egg for him to use after graduating college.

JS's father was a self made man who escaped a hard working but impoverished ghetto with a ravenous appetite for education and an innate knowledge that there had to be MORE. Nothing was ever enough, there was always MORE to be had! More wealth, more security, more knowledge, more everything.

As a result, when JS was born, his father made sure to drill into him that no matter what external forces were at play, there was no limit to what he could achieve.

JS's degree landed him a position as an aide to a senior staffer who supported, nurtured and cultivated his creativity and economic prowess. JS came to the table with his first financial 'set point' being to land a $50k per year job by the time he was 28. He's currently 27 and just landed that job. His next 'set point' is to make six figures by the time he's 35. After that, he will have the investments, capital and contacts to build his own company. He wants to retire by 60 with an 8 figure annual income.

The odds are, he will achieve a huge amount of the success he has been programmed to, if not all of it.

Very rarely does the difference between success and struggle come down to the intellectual prowess of an individual. It is, in fact, our programming to a large degree that even determines our learning power, the limits of our intellect.

Knowns – whether they are good or bad for us, we will choose them at every possible instance, so long as we are acting without conscious direction, and sometimes even when we think we are, we still choose a negative-effect known over an unknown.

Why does a smoker continue to smoke even when they know it's not good for them? Because they KNOW what to expect when they light the cigarette, they KNOW the first cough will come right after the first drag, they KNOW the back of their throat will sear with chemical fire burning through the mucous membrane leaving the tissue weakened and stressed and eventually subject to the cancer that will set up shop in his/her throat.

Unknowns – Knowing is only half of the problem, the other half of the problem is the fact that what will happen to the smoker when they quit is an UNKNOWN. They DON'T KNOW how they will feel in the morning, they DON'T KNOW what they will do while they have that first cup of coffee. They DON'T KNOW how it's going to feel being able to run up or down the stairs without being winded. They DON'T KNOW what they're going to do with the money they're not putting toward cigarettes!

Fear of UNKNOWNS drives the subconscious homeostatic program even when the results of a known behavior are detrimental to the well being of our organism as a whole.

The self-sabotaging exec who can't break past $40k per year doesn't know what it's like to be a millionaire, and subconsciously doesn't WANT to know!

$40k per year is comfortable; the status, the purchasing power, it's all KNOWN. What will happen if they suddenly made $50k a year is UNKNOWN. The program that anyone who makes more than $40k per year is 'too big for their britches' or 'THAT kind of people' coupled with internalized negative connotation keeps the individual's Wealth Set Point at $40k per year.

All the information contained here is simply meant to provide an alternative view, and a few coping strategies that may help others find the way to their own life of wellness, satisfaction and fulfillment that all sentient beings are entitled to.

My life, like yours is a work in progress. Like all people, I too experience good times and bad times. One of the most important keys to building a life of satisfaction and fulfillment is to keep the bad times reduced to the barest possible minimum while increasing the duration of the good times to their maximum potential. Add this to the number of things you have in your life that bring you joy, and what you have, in the language of Power, is a multi-phase source for fulfillment, that source is YOUR mindset, is it a "growth" mindset? Or is yours a "fixed" mindset? (Look up Carol Dweck + Fixed mindset vs. Growth mindset on Youtube). It all starts with YOU.

Rather than filling these pages with the same old hashed and rehashed bits let's get them out in the open now so that you are able to decide just how ready you are to move forward.

There is no right, and no wrong, there is no; "You must do this now". All these steps are yours to take or leave at the convenience of your life. The most important part is that with this information, you are armed for a life you are worthy of, at whatever time you choose to begin.

The following is a list of physical equipment you will need to begin your journey.

Pen.

Calendar.

The following is a list of emotional equipment you will need to begin your journey.

Belief – that you are worthy of a fulfilling and satisfying life.

Desire – to build that life.

Expectation – that you can do anything you set your mind to!

Determination – to stand against those who would sabotage your efforts, (including you), no matter what ghosts, insecurities and past failures they may dredge up and throw into your face.

The most important thing to know about making changes from who you were programmed by others to be, to the you who's going to write their own new life program is PERMISSION.

That permission can only come from one source. You.

I'm here to open your eyes to your own potential. It's a gift that was given to me by my mother, and one I hope to pass forward.

As we did when we were children, let's start with the ABC's and 123's.

These are the building blocks to your successful recovery of who you are meant to be.

A) Acknowledge, and most importantly ACCEPT that you are worthy of self-direction and fulfillment.

This means you'll often come face to face with the indoctrinations others have used to stifle, control and manipulate you all of your life.

It's at this point that you'll need to decide whether or not you're going to keep the ideals, ideas and programming others used to make you into who they wanted you to be, or if you're going to rewrite your own program to be who YOU want to be. You will also need to decide, as you inspect the 'code' of your programming what you find worth keeping and what needs to be re-written. Only you can do this, only you have the RIGHT to do this.

B) Budget.

Budget your resources (the computer, family, friends), budget your money, and most importantly budget your TIME! Set aside whatever time you need each week to pursue the person you feel you are meant to be.

C) Create a plan.

Use a notebook, calendar, calculator, get a list of those who have succeeded before you, together. Set a time frame. i.e. by next week I'll have 5 letters of introduction ready to go to my potential mentors. In one year I'll be an apprentice, in two years I'll be in "x" position, ten years after that I'll have "xxx" resources, income, and position...

Any self-help 'guru' will tell you that writing down your goals dramatically increases your chances of success. Why, you might ask? Simple. You're training your subconscious to accept changes to its programming. Writing is an ideo-motor activity. Once we have learned the mechanics of writing and have developed our handwriting style, the actual use of cursive becomes subconscious. We can address our own subconscious mind by writing out our goals, and seeing them in our own writing. By doing this, we open the filter of our mind to the possibilities of achieving those goals, slowly turning them from Unknowns to Knowns, effectively reprogramming ourselves to a new level of personal achievement in any endeavor. The Kappas Mental Bank system is one of the most consistently successful models of this kind of personal reprogramming.

When you look at the happenings in the world around you, ask yourself why they don't teach children cursive anymore. Could it be that by utilizing a writing system that helps GROW the brain and its concurrent neuropathways we would be raising smarter children, those more capable of critical thinking, those more capable of questioning the status quo? Could it be that there are those who hold the reins to our society that would want to make sure that the children who are coming up in this world don't have the mental capacity to question them? Or question why things are done the way they are? Cursive is a tool that stimulates thinking, if your child's school won't teach it, perhaps you might think about teaching your child yourself.

Now for the 123's

1) Research whatever is necessary to achieve your goals. Is it more education? Is it more money? Is it more time? How much will you need to devote? How long will it take? What are reasonable expectations given what will be required?

2) Secure your mentor. Your mentor should be someone who has achieved what you aspire to have or be. Most people, once they have achieved their own measure of success are very happy to help the next 'generation' do the same. Being able to pay our achievements forward

helps assure us that our own efforts will not be forgotten even if one day our name is.

3) Take the first step. After all the research and leg work you've done, you now know what to do. All you have to do, is actually do it. So do it. Take the first step of your journey.

What follows are 10 Simple Steps that can help you stay on task as you re-write your program and become the person you know you were always meant to be.

"The chief cause of human error is to be found in prejudices picked up in childhood." – Descartes

What do you want to be when you grow up?

It's one of the first questions we learn to answer with any kind of actual thought. It's also one of the first questions whose answer gives us a sometimes blistering understanding of how others look at us, judge us, and what exactly they may or may not come to value about us.

This is the question upon whose answer we learn to give others control of our "self" esteem.

Take a moment to go back to the beginning of the above question and ask your childhood self, "What do you want to be when you grow up?"

Listen to that child's answer, if you're anything like I was, you wanted to be a doctor, a firefighter, a veterinarian, a cowgirl (or boy), a police officer, a soldier, an astronaut, a time traveler, or all of the above all at once, and you couldn't see any reason why you might not be able to attain all of those things.

I've never met a person who said, "I wanna be a heroin addict when I grow up." Or "I wanna be a suicidal manic depressive who jumps in front of a bus," or "I wanna be like the homeless guy passed out in front of the liquor store," or, well you get the idea.

Now, go ahead and put the dark side aside for a while, and sit with that child who wants to be that firefighter, doctor, etc. and think about the child you used to be, THAT child. See if you can remember a time when you knew who you were without some adult telling you who they saw you as. Now, ask that child WHY you wanted to be any of those 'things'. What drew you to it?

I'm not going to even begin to list the possibilities here, the idea is for YOU to honestly answer the question of what drew you to that particular 'idea'. HINT: There are no right or wrong answers. The truth of 'power' is just as valid as the truth of 'to be someone to look up to', it's your action in the face of that truth that becomes the greater insight into your nature, and I personally am in no position to judge, honestly, neither are you.

When you can answer the question, 'why' then it's entirely possible you have forged the first connection back to that child and the idea he or she had about what those 'icons' meant, and what exactly, that means to you.

Oddly enough, the same can be said for the child who wants to 'rule the world' or 'be the richest person in the world' or any such extravagance. Ask the question 'why' and when the honest, naked answer makes itself known, you will be one step closer to the truth of your own nature.

Did you grow up impoverished? Did you, like Scarlett O'Hara vow to "Never go hungry again!" and so wealth and the accumulation of it became your ruling obsession?

Did you grow up with enough of everything including love so that you wanted to find a way to make other people feel what you had, and because of that desire thought, "I'll be a social worker!" Then perhaps later on you chose a 'practical' career (usually at the encouragement of pragmatic family members), that kept you financially secure but emotionally unfulfilled? Some people say "that's where hobbies come in."

Hobbies are great. They help us keep our sanity, but, let me ask you this, if you could wake up every day and look forward to what you do, if you could wake up every day and WANT to go to work because you love what you do, not because you're trying to escape a horrible home life, or not because you think 'if I work hard enough today I might get that raise', how much more happiness do you think you'd have in your life?

30% more? Since work is approximately 30% of our life, I'd say that's a reasonable estimate.

If you could go to a job that you loved doing, that let you come home at night, or at 3 in the morning, or whenever, but left you feeling full on that back shelf on the inside of your heart, even if you had only a cup of beans and 2 eggs to eat for dinner, how would you feel about that?

What is, where is, the line for your trade off? Who drew it, you or someone who disapproved of your childhood dream of being a wandering circus veterinarian? Why?

It's true that sometimes we get accustomed to a particular lifestyle, a stationary house instead of a motor home, a house instead of an apartment, a 4 door, 6 or 8 cylinder luxury car vs. a 2 door, 4 cylinder hybrid. Changing that lifestyle against our will is very uncomfortable. But what happens when you intentionally make those changes and begin to seek out that which makes you happy; filling that shelf with satisfying deeds that honor the nature you were destined for before someone else put *their* ideas and ideals into your head and changed who you COULD be, into someone THEY thought *you* SHOULD be?

What if you, as the person you are today, went back to observe the truth of that personal nature. Could you imagine finding something you do in your present life that could lead you to the fulfillment that nature craves?

Before you answer that question, consider this one, have you ever failed? Did you survive it? Apply that to what you feel might happen if you do not honor that 'thing', that part of your nature, will you survive it? I'll bet the answer is 'Yes'.

Now consider what might happen if you found that 'thing' that led you to fulfillment and succeeded in nothing other than honoring it. Might it be possible that you would find or add joy to your life? I'll bet the answer is 'Yes'.

Are you ready?

The Happiness Formula

The happiness formula is simple. If H (Happiness) = >70% of emotional content at least 70% of the time then one can be considered generally happy.

Period.

Weigh it. Balance it. Budget it. Can you say that at least 70% of the time you are happy? If so, then, as my grandmother used to say, you have blessings on you and your house!

If not, then, it is time to find and start that first thing that can tip the scales.

"I always wanted to be a fireman, I can't physically do it, I can't do the work…"

Learn how to be a fire prevention inspector. Take a class on it, teach a class on it. Learn about combustion. Obtain knowledge about that which draws you, and figure out how to share it. Contact local section 8 housing, or low income housing authorities and offer to give fire prevention tips, as well as basic use of extinguishers etc. Chances are, if you start moving toward what inspires you, you will continue to do so, and someone will understand what you need to give, and they will help you find a way to give it. That is THEIR need, their drive and it needs to be respected just as much as yours does.

(Yes, if you're into cadavers learn about embalming, or whatever part of death enthralls you, just please don't become a serial killer, perhaps use your intellect and information to help them stop before they take more innocent victims.)

Your right to pursue happiness and fulfillment must never be allowed or used to obstruct or harm another.

1. Own Your Past, Forgive, but don't Forget

Forgive, forget ... what's the difference?

There are many folks who will tell you that forgiving means forgetting, these people are not ready to understand that forgiving means the opposite, that in fact, forgiving means accepting, in spite of...

Forgiving means trying to understand where a perceived transgression comes from, and accepting it as part of the transgressors' nature.

What one person (you) perceives as a transgression or hurtful act may well be a common response from the one who hurt you, and therefore by that person, is not perceived as hurtful.

It is up to you to determine whether or not you're willing to continue accepting responses that cause pain.

If you decide you are willing to continue accepting responses from others that cause pain, doubt, fear, anxiety, or reduced self-esteem, reduced-personal sovereignty, then you must be prepared to accept the consequences of pain, doubt, fear, anxiety, reduced self-esteem and reduced personal sovereignty. There is no getting around this fact.

If you wish to accept someone else's judgment of your worth, then you have (until such a time as you reclaim your right), given your esteem to someone else to measure and value or devalue according to THEIR yardstick instead of your own.

Forgiving frequently means examining, weighing, and accepting something that it may very well be contrary to YOUR personal nature to accept. Forgiving requires knowledge of the person, and the reasonings behind their actions, as well as a deep knowledge of self, usually revolving around whether or not you're in a position to make changes that you desire.

Forgiveness also means frequently extending your own ability to empathize or sympathize with someone else and whatever may have been plaguing them at the moment they lashed out

For those who argue that forgiveness equates to forgetting, I tell you here and now that this is not so. Forgetting a perceived transgression is virtually impossible when it accompanies personal pain, it is too connected to the person who hurt you. Forgiving is a vastly different state of mind, and one that it is essential to bring into the home of your heart.

You can forgive without forgetting. In fact you should not forget. To paraphrase the immortal words of Santayana, "Those who forget the past are usually doomed to repeat it." Truer words have never been quoted or mis-quoted.

Forgetting a transgression against your self, your sovereignty, your person is the same as denying that any such event ever happened. If that is a choice you enter into willingly and with knowledge and understanding, that is certainly your choice. If it is a mindset you are encouraged to take at the behest of someone else then it is one you'd do well to think over several times.

Forgetting leaves a door open for others to commit the same transgression against you. Forgiving leaves the door open for you to make more well educated choices about who you let influence your life, based on the experiences of the past.

Would you choose to have amnesia and perhaps waste time living all your 'programming mistakes' again or would you prefer to walk into the light, educated, accepting of the mistakes you've made, and knowing that you are armed for better decisions to create a future that is true to your nature?

Who Are You? (This is your space).

2. Claim Ownership of Your Future.

"The faults of a superior person are like the sun and moon. They have their faults, and everyone sees them; they change and everyone looks up to them." - Confucius[1]

Stand Up to Your Past

This is always easier to do once you have faced and owned it.

Your past is the weapon your detractors will use against you, to try and dissuade you from making positive changes. Your past is what your own inner voice will throw into your face to remind you of previous "failures", or those moments when you were less than perfect.

This is the time to acknowledge a realization and take a vow.

The realization: Perfection is an inherently unattainable state.

The vow: The idea of "perfection" will have to be modified to one of EXCELLENCE.

Perfection is unattainable, whether you subscribe to a religion or dogmatic belief system or not, the only perfection that exists is numeric. We, as sentient, cognizant beings have a creative, rationalizing, capacity that allows variances in accordance with the rational mind's attempts to quantify emotional and perceptive experience, these variances, in and of themselves disallow the idea of perfection as something within the realm of human experience.

Excellence however, is dependent upon the moment, the circumstances and any number of Newtonian and quantum variables, therefore excellence is an outcome to be aspired to, always within the constraints of the moment and all its applied variables. Within those variables, a

---

1. http://www.brainyquote.com/quotes/quotes/c/confucius398494.html

state of excellence is utterly achievable thanks to its very mutability, whereas striving for perfection is a setup for certain failure.

Are You Who You Want to Be?

If "Yes." Great.

If "Yes, but…" Even better.

If "No." Then let's get going.

The first thing you should know is that your friends, family and closest confidantes will most likely be all too eager to help you sabotage your attempts to live a life that's truer to who YOU are. Just as your body has its own homeostatic set point, (the point of healthful balance where everything is running and functioning as it should), so do your friends and family, and like it or not, you, as you are, or as they've programmed you to be, are part of *their* homeostasis.

It's like when you go on a diet, they'll pat you on the back and say, "That's great! Let me know how I can help! Hey you wanna go out for happy hour?" It's not that they're necessarily intentionally sabotaging you, or setting the stage for you to sabotage yourself, (sometimes that's true) but the truth is it's more likely they don't even necessarily realize what they're doing or what effect it'll have on you. This is where you need to make sure you're acting consciously, and actively choosing the unknown over the known.

So, very much like when dieting, this re-defined life you're building, this Truer version of yourself is done from within, and the odds are you will be far more successful if you take care about those you share your goals with, accountability should always be maintained with yourself. If you fall off, or "slip up" in the dieter's vernacular, accept it and move forward, it really IS that simple.

The whole point is that you don't need permission to be true to yourself. None of us ever did, we've just been conditioned, indoctrinated, and programmed all throughout history to THINK we did. It's time to wake up and be the person it makes YOU happy to be, and from you, others will learn that they too are entitled to this miraculous gift. You will become the light to show the way.

3. Identify and Define Exactly Who You Want To Be.

Competition

"If a man does not keep pace with his companions, perhaps it is because he hears a different drummer. Let him step to the music he hears, however measure or far away." – Henry David Thoreau[1]

It is the nature of human kind to grow through challenge and competition. How many of us haven't ever heard the phrase, "keeping up with the Joneses," in reference to getting that new house, or new car, or newest satellite or techno gizmo? Have you ever asked yourself why? What does this focus on someone else's state of existence truly have to do with you or the satisfaction you garner from your own? Why should your measure of self come from what someone else has or doesn't have? Because that's what corporations, advertisers and the media have programmed us to believe.

Every time you turn on the television you're confronted with happy, beautiful people who have things you want. Advertising is nothing more than programming associations into your subconscious, very like a hypnotist who, with your permission helps you reprogram yourself to allow the changes you seek, to actually take place.

Advertising uses sight, sound and sympathy to achieve its objective, inundating the individual with literal, subliminal and fantastical (as in fantasy) images. Catchy jingles create brain-worms, and particular colors access particular areas of our brain to drive action. Typically reds, oranges, yellows, (warm colors) can spur a person to physical action, raising blood pressure and temperature, whereas blues and cool colors

---

1. http://www.boardofwisdom.com/

   default.asp?topic=1010&search=Henry+David+Thorea

   u

have the opposite effect, usually implying relaxation, recreation and low energy endeavors. Once you become aware of how the media is programming you, you can make the best choices based on empirical data rather than emotionally charged manipulations. You'll be surprised what you discover once you start paying attention to the gimmicks.

Fact is, advertising and media is one of the most deeply rooted transgressions against individuality and self-determination that exists.

The measure of the individual, against themselves, as the person they are versus the person they Want To Be, is the only genuine measure that matters.

It's a very hard fact to swallow, and one that many people won't want to. It's so much easier to compare yourself, your have's and haven't's to someone else, it's so much easier to blame someone else for what you don't have than to admit the cause of your lack lies in your own program. The one thing you must know about this state of existence is this: We all do it.

The only harm in living this way is the harm that comes to the self; that harm is geometrically multiplied once an individual realizes that the only person responsible for their life is their self, AND that individual continues to lay blame where it does not belong.

In 2006 a book called "The Secret" by Rhonda Byrne was published. It took the world by storm, promising that the "Law of Attraction" (being, 'what you put out to the universe will come back on you') if used properly, will result in your happiness, success and bliss.

In a way, the entire book is a huge oversimplification, and yet, it can work, it can work because as soon as you set your mind to a task or an achievement, your subconscious begins to puzzle out how to attain or obtain your objective. It frequently fails because the surface tenet of "live like you have what you want" as the interpretation of cause, fails.

Consider that it may be inaccurately interpreted. Instead perhaps the tenet should be: "Live like you ARE who you WANT to be."

Change begins within and the Law of Attraction, REQUIRES action.

Basic philosophy holds that if you are not satisfied with who you are, and what you see in the mirror, then it is YOU who must begin to make the changes necessary.

In screenwriting we use an external antagonist or set of circumstances to FORCE our 'hero' (this would be you in the movie of your life) to break free of his status quo, slog his way through the mire of 'rational' actions until every one of them has failed, leaving the 'hero' no other choice but to embrace change and BECOME what he must in order to succeed against the bad guys.

Reality is rarely so dramatic. Most of us slog our way through the mire of rational actions over and over, failing over and over again until we just give up. That's the sad truth. It's not that we're not capable of becoming the hero we want to be, it's that we don't know how to use the tools we have to make the change. We think we need that outside force to push us into becoming the 'hero' but when that happens, we resent it. And since our movie never ends until we do, we're stuck being what others want us to be. No matter what we try, or what the testimonials tell us have worked for so many others, we only find the results, when it comes to ourselves, to be less than stellar or simply temporary as we backslide into our original program.

Contrary to what you might think, this is NOT failure, this is evidence of our 'script' working PERFECTLY.

If you want to be the hero of the movie of your life, then you MUST change your script!

It starts with thought, and that frequently starts with asking hard questions and facing even harder answers. Preferably those answers come from within *you* and not from the dogmas, expectations and voiced disappointments of those around you. Quieting the voices of others so that your own can be heard is one of the hardest things you'll ever do.

Once you know who and what you want to be, the next step is to find yourself a mentor.

Your mentor will almost always be someone who came before you and managed to accomplish exactly what you're wanting to do for yourself. Most people who have achieved their goals love sharing how they did it.

It seems to be a fairly general rule of those who attain success that there is a need to pass on the way in which they achieved what they have. This is true for every kind of success there is, from spiritual to corporate, everyone who succeeds in living this life is driven to pass forward the things they deem most important for continuing that success within another generation. It's the same reason we are compelled to pass on our genes as a species, passing this information forward becomes our own brand of immortality.

Who do you want to be? (This is your space too.)

4. Set Reasonable Goals

"The journey of a thousand miles begins with a single step." – Confucius

Once you've broken your goals down into small manageable steps, it's much easier to begin walking the path that honors your true self.

Real Life Gets in the Way

"But I can't just do what I want... I have obligations!"

Odds are, you do. I do too, and yet my first obligation is to myself. Without honoring myself, I am incapable of truly honoring those around me. If I cannot pursue my passion, I cannot be genuinely happy for someone else who IS pursuing their passion.

In all fairness I am extremely lucky and very grateful! I have a 'day job' that is incredibly fulfilling, and I'm lucky enough to work with an outstanding group of people. I'm also lucky enough to have a wonderful clientele, most of whom prefer to find the silver lining, even in their misfortunes than to dwell in the darkness of them. Everybody knows negativity is contagious. One person's bad mood can affect everyone's IF you let it, but why should you?

Why should you allow yourself to be victimized by someone else's pessimism? You shouldn't. It's hard not to let someone else's mood affect you, but it's worth the effort to try.

Instead, remind yourself of all the great things you have or the great things you're building into your life and remember that someone else's troubles are not yours to bear. You're not a pack mule for someone else's baggage.

You can be sympathetic, and empathetic, but you cannot run their life. It is up to the individual to WANT to change what's wrong in their life, you can't do it for them. What you can do, is lead by example whenever possible.

When someone tries to infuse your mood with negativity you can politely decline to converse on the subject, or politely remove yourself from the area. You can choose to let yourself become mired in trouble or you can choose to focus on those things you have control over; yourself and your own attitude.

One of the most obvious times this kind of situation occurs is with family during holidays. The people who push your buttons, forcing you to push theirs back are exactly the kind of "known's", or known behaviors that it's hardest to break from. But what if you did? What if you chose the Unknown avenue of letting someone spout whatever they could just to get a rise out of you and not giving them the satisfaction of it? Or if you're the meek and mild one who keeps your mouth shut to 'keep the peace', what if you did voice your opinion but managed to keep it positive? It's Unknown, but so was the Western World once.

The first strategy of de-stressing your holiday distress, is to accept that the people who push your buttons do so, because it's in their script, or their program. You have always reacted the way you did because of YOUR program but now you are in the midst of rewriting it. You have more power than they think, and it's your duty to yourself to think and act as the person whose program you're writing, rather than reacting as the one whose script THEY wrote. This is your power, your holiday, you've lived through the drama before, you know each person's script, you know their characters, their flaws, their strengths and you now know your own. Having this information gives you the psychological shield called objectivity. You can now use your conscious knowledge to deflect attacks against yourself (as long as you own your past, it cannot be used as a weapon against you), and to rise above the desire to retaliate.

You have the power to accept that those around you are only acting in perfect accordance with their life scripts or their programming, but you are free to make active choices in your behavior rather than deal with the aftermath of knee-jerk reactions. This is your power. This is you, leading by example.

5. Health Matters.

"Let your food be your medicine, and your medicine be your food."
Hippocrates.

Be Your Own Health Care Advocate.

Your body is your "temple" your "palace" your "vehicle", whichever fits your concept of it, know that you and only you are responsible for gaining and maintaining your health. Many can aid you in your quest for health, but only you can perform the acts necessary.

When I was a young girl, I can easily recall having conversations with various family members about diseases and cures. Usually these conversations took place around the time I was due for school required vaccinations, and though there was a negative experience behind my assertion that I didn't need vaccines, there was a deeper belief at the center of my so-called argument.

The belief I'm talking about was a single simple 'gut instinct' that whatever disease nature created or allowed to exist, nature could cure too.

The negative experience I'm about to share will probably be considered almost comedic by some, but consider both the mindset of a middle aged doctor, as well as the mindset of a 7 year old female in the 1970's.

At seven years old, a normal child is self-aware. Within the realm of their experiences so far, they know what they like and what they don't. By seven years old the odds are a child has learned at least some basics of etiquette, proper behavior, and modesty. Also by seven years old many children have at least a rudimentary understanding of what respect is, both for self and for others.

Taking the above statements into consideration, and the fact that pediatricians are doctors who specialize in children, consider the following true story, then consider how you would feel if it'd been your experience, or your child's.

In the mid 1970's I was brought to the doctor for a booster shot before starting the school year. It wasn't the shot I had a problem with, it was the fact that I had to pull my pants down, in front of someone else, to receive it.

At this age I was already subject to teasing both from family and peers about being chubby, and as a result of that I became extremely modest, especially when the situation was out of my control.

So, sitting in the doctor's office with my mom, I decided that the shot would be administered in my arm rather than butt. So when the doctor called my name, I stood tall and confident and told him where he could stick the needle.

His reply was something along the lines of, "that's not how it works, this one goes in your tush."

To which I, as a precocious child replied, "then I just won't get it." Or some such thing.

At this point the doctor simply pulled my pants down and gave me the shot in the rump. We were still in the waiting room.

It was a moment of humiliation that forty years later I still recall with obscene clarity. All in the name of a booster shot, my personal sovereignty was violated and I was literally stripped bare bottomed in front of 'the world'.

Now, all things being equal there are many children who regularly suffer much more horrifying indignities than this could ever be seen as. But given this tiny little indignity (I cried as if I'd been beaten, and my mother never brought me back to that doctor just so you know), all it takes is a little imagination to develop sympathy and empathy for all those kids out there who are regularly victimized by people that are supposed to protect them.

There are a few points to the above story: the first being that the doctor didn't even try to explain that it was more effective or efficient to give a booster shot in the butt. Maybe he thought I was too young to understand but the odds are that he, being a white male in his 60's at the time, was probably not keen on the idea of being questioned by a seven year old female.

Some may see that as a grand assumption on my part but if you didn't live through the 70's and experience the mindsets and mentalities of those who came of age before then, you can't understand what I'm saying.

In the 70's doctors were still considered by many to be about as close to Gods as a human could get without being some kind of clergyman. After all, doctors knew about the body, how it worked and they had the reputation for saving lives.

Dr. Kildare, Ben Casey, Marcus Welby M.D. are just a few examples of the "Doctor as near God" in popular culture.

M.A.S.H. – the show about a surgical team in war torn Korea was a groundbreaker not just because it tackled so many pertinent issues from women's rights to bigotry to addiction; but because in spite of the fact that these medical professionals frequently performed surgical miracles, they were written and portrayed as deeply flawed HUMAN BEINGS just trying to do the best they could to help others while living in impossible circumstances.

What's the point of all of the above?

Doctors, are just people.

They're trained in the workings of the human body and how to fix things that go wrong, especially when it comes to trauma. Most of them are excellent when it comes to handling the mechanics of traumatic effect.

What more than 95% of Medical Doctors are NOT good at, is prevention, maintenance and relating to their patients.

A hugely disproportionate amount of class time for a doctor is spent on biochemistry, honestly so they can learn more accurately how and what to prescribe to their patients to keep them and their conditions "managed".

Check out who subsidizes medical schools, and where grants come from.

The Pharmaceutical industry is a multi-billion-dollar per WEEK-business. Chemo 'therapeutic' agents alone, in America, are estimated to earn pharmaceutical companies upwards of 4 billion dollars per week. (This is an obscenely conservative estimate.)

The fact is, pharmaceutical companies don't want people cured. They want people and their conditions 'managed', they want sick people kept alive and their conditions controlled *enough* so that they can continue working. If they're able to continue working, they can continue paying for their meds. Then, as the meds become less effective at controlling the condition, and symptoms return or grow worse, more meds are introduced with a whole extra slew of possible side effects that need to be managed by more drugs made by the same pharmaceutical companies. It's a controlled spiral descent that leads to people in their

60's, 70's and 80's (often living on fixed incomes...when was the last time you heard of a senior citizen or retiree that was actually enjoying their retirement and the fruits of their life long labors rather than fighting to stave off the effects of chronic conditions?) frequently requiring multiple medications, at multiple times a day, to manage symptoms rather than cure the diseases they do have.

Historically speaking, in America there have been at least a dozen researchers, doctors, and biochemists that have developed cures for everything from diabetes, to heart disease, to almost every kind of cancer. The powers that be, here in America have done everything they can, from harassment to manufacturing and disseminating false information, to discredit them and chase them out of the country. After all, there's approximately FOUR BILLION DOLLARS PER WEEK at stake.

So when it comes down to someone, anyone who suggests that a better, healthier life can be yours for the taking simply by treating your personal organism as a WHOLE and feeding it the appropriate fuel, (instead of hyper processed "foods" laden with sugar and high fructose corn syrup), they are ridiculed, called hippies, or crackpots, and most certainly blacklisted among the medical and pharmaceutical establishment.

Again, taking all of the above into consideration, there are times when medicines are wholly appropriate and necessary, but you don't take antibiotics for a cold and any doctor that prescribes them to you for one isn't holding up their end of the Hippocratic Oath. A cold is caused by a virus, antibiotics are effective against bacterial agents NOT viruses.

One last word on doctors, most of them get into medicine because they are driven for some reason, to help.

Yes it's lucrative once they pay off the couple hundred thousand dollars in debt, but for the most part doctors and medical practitioners do deserve the same respect that every other living creature deserves.

So, with regards to your health, if you are interested in keeping it, you have to bear the responsibility for re-gaining and maintaining it.

This is just a part of my personal journey as well.

We've grown accustomed to the idea that a "cure" is a one time thing, (pill, IV, shot, etc) and that once the "cure" is administered, we can go back to the habits that created the situation in the first place. Nothing could be farther from the truth.

The cure is nothing more difficult, or simple than restructuring the habits that created the situation in the first place.

Taking care of your body with healthy fuel can and will change your life, your health, your mental clarity, your longevity, well, EVERY aspect, from your energy levels, to your sexual prowess will skyrocket, and instead of feeling bogged down and bloaty in the belly, your steps will be filled with a vigor you probably haven't had since your teen years.

Now... let's build a foundation for your new life.

Self-Medication

Most of us do it with food. Many of us do it with drink. Lots of others do it with drugs whether legal or illegal.

I was the kid who ate powdered sugar out of the box, it's only now, forty years later, that I understand why. The blood sugar ups and downs, the effect all those empty calories had on my happiness-hormones and the fact that I could stuff myself until I wanted to puke, but never felt satisfied.

There are so many things that go into the feeling of satiety that there are books and movies and documentaries made about it all. So for this work I'll simply re-state a couple things that are available for the finding out in the electronic world.

You can eat 3 lbs of fast food and never be truly satisfied, you may be stuffed, but your body will not be nourished.

OR

You can eat 3 lbs of nutritionally dense food and be set until your next regular meal.

Why the difference? Nutritional content is one of the factors, your body simply can't squeeze enough nutrition out of the fast food to keep it running well, all it's able to pull out is fat and high fructose corn syrup that makes you 'high' for a little while. Your stomach has nutrient receptors in it that determine when you have consumed enough nutrients, (minerals, vitamins, phytochemicals, etc.) for the time being, so that it signals you're satisfied. When you don't get the quantity of nutrients you need to function optimally (like what comes out of fast food or highly processed food), you can actually gorge and starving yourself all at the same time, which is why you never really feel satisfied when eating junk food

One of the other factors is simply stretch receptors in the stomach. When you put a proper amount of nutritionally dense food, the fact is, you need less of it to fuel yourself and stay satiated.

So the first thing you must consider, if you're serious about taking control of your health is to switch the kind of fuel you're giving your vehicle.

Give it a shot, challenge yourself for three weeks to eat nothing but products that are a single step away from how they were grown.

Above all else, give your body a chance to rest and recover from the processed and specialty beverages.

Try eating like this for 21 days, note how you feel, how much energy you have, whether or not you NEED a nap in the afternoon or just want to enjoy one. If you don't note positive changes in your personal palace you can always go back to making the fast food corporations richer.

6. Stress Management

"Give yourself to the dark side, it is the only way to save your friends..."
Darth Vader

Drawn to the Dark Side

We're indoctrinated to the idea that the sacrifice of self is the most noble act we can commit. In certain situations, i.e. the defense of another, taking a stand for the betterment of society, etc., that can be true, but in most of the situations each of us will encounter in our daily lives, it is a grotesque falsehood.

How can a parent raise a child that has not only respect for his/herself but for others too, if the parent never shows respect for themselves or their needs? The denial of your own needs as a human being, in order to satisfy the 'sacrificial requirement' of being a parent frequently leaves people burnt out and desperate. It also teaches, in particular, your female children, that their needs don't matter when pitted up against someone else's. Though it's a strong message, in my opinion it's not the right one.

There is, of course, also a dark side to self-care, it can degenerate into hedonism and the far too prevalent, 'hooray for me, to hell with you' attitude we see everywhere from the political arena to public venues. The media doesn't help.

Avoiding the dark side is as simple and as difficult as finding and maintaining balance. When you care for, nurture, and honor yourself, you set the example for your friends and family that they are worthy of granting themselves the same respect. When your friends and family are competent in tending their own needs, then the capacity and ability to nurture each other becomes a joy instead of a duty.

Fear, Doubt

These two conditions are the anchors of the dark side, their aim is to weigh down the lofty ambitions we have for ourselves and keep us 'grounded' in 'reality'.

Both of these conditions are spawned from outside of us and internalized frequently before we take our first steps. The internalization of the doubts and fears of others follows us and is reinforced all throughout our lives by teachers, parents, siblings, and well-meaning friends who "don't want you to get hurt".

Have you ever seen a child reach for something on a hot stove only to have his or her hand slapped away, only so they can try again and get slapped away again? There was a time when a parent would let a child get near enough to feel the heat. Then the child would have learned not to touch, or to be extremely careful. Nowadays that kind of parenting is a rare thing. Children are no longer encouraged to learn, they are fed answers rather than taught how to find them, much of this is due to the 'fear' that a child may be held back, or the 'doubt' that they are capable of learning, or learning how to learn.

For parents there's also the fear and doubt combined that their child or children will be left behind or won't be able to keep up with 'Suzy' or 'Billy' or any of the other 'Jones''. The fear that if kids are given the chance to be children and to learn according to their own strengths and in their own time that they'll miss out on opportunities the *parents* FEAR will never come again. So instead of appreciating the child for who they are, they're frequently pushed, prodded and medicated into a Stepford oblivion in order to force them to conform to parameters that were dictated by someone else. If this sounds familiar, you're starting to recognize the program.

Every one of us needs to decide whether or not we're willing to perpetuate this program. Do you want something truly, organically, holistically better for your children, or will the status quo do?

These same questions can and should be asked of each of us with regards to what we want for ourselves. The only time it's too late to change is when we're six feet under.

Hope, Faith

These are the flip-side of fear and doubt. They require a literal shift in focus from the potential negatives of their antitheses to the potential positive outcomes you're able to visualize or imagine by becoming the person you were meant to be. These are the core qualities of your life story's hero. When a negative impulse or thought comes to mind, it must intentionally be countered with positivity born of both hope and faith. In time, that negative impulse (like the playground bully who you stood up to all those years ago) will learn, it has no place in your life, and it will cease to be.

It ain't always easy, but it is always worthwhile.

7. Do What You Love.

"You've got to find what you love. And that is as true for your work as it is for your lovers. Your work is going to fill a large part of your life, and the only way to be truly satisfied is to do what you believe is great work. And the only way to do great work is to love what you do. If you haven't found it yet, keep looking, don't settle!" – Steve Jobs

Start Small

The above quote was eventually distilled down to one we're all familiar with; "Do what you love, the money will follow".

Once again, thanks to oversimplification the true message has gotten lost. I can't help but wonder if this is a conscious or unconscious side effect of our nature. In our quest for a memorable sound byte the nuances of language get lost, and the entire meaning of a statement or phrase changes. The true damage that this will cause to our species and our continuing acquisition and transmission of knowledge, in the long run won't be able to be determined any time soon.

It takes small steps to create a solid foundation. Each stone, brick and board must be carefully placed and secured before anything else can be built. Tend to the details to create a superior vision for yourself and those you love, it's those details that eventually create the big picture.

Be Mindful

It's really not about controlling every thought. It's about keeping our minds on the thoughts we WANT to give our energy to.

Thought energy is creative energy, and creative energy is the currency of your life, and the universe is your one stop shop.

But it's still up to you to find the best bargain for your energetic buck and this is where mindfulness really plays the biggest part in the creation of your life.

To go back to the shopping analogy, mindfulness is like walking into the grocery store with your list in hand, whereas letting your mind go where it wants is simply meandering through the store knowing you have to make something but having no concept of what that might be.

It's your opportunity to focus on the power of your intention and intention is the energy that breeds manifestation through mindfulness.

Set a goal that you can believe you can achieve within a certain time frame.

For instance, "By next quarter I want to double my sales numbers."

If you're a small business owner, you might have a plan now to do that by refining your target demographic and cutting the advertising fat that doesn't produce.

If you're a sales person on the floor of a store, you might decide to start meandering the store looking for people to engage rather than just hanging out at the register waiting for people to come to you.

In the movie The Pursuit of Happyness, Will Smith plays a man so down on his luck that he's living in a public restroom with his son. When he finally scores a job he sets about strategically utilizing his time to ensure he succeeds to the level of his best expectation. He comes in early, stays later than most and doesn't hang up the phone between calls, all of which saves him time and earns him higher sales rankings than his peers. In the end (spoiler) he succeeds. He succeeds because he focuses on what he wants and doesn't allow himself to get distracted from what will lead him to success. He focuses his energy.

Focusing your energy on your success, and exercising mindfulness about what you really want, (is it really financial security you want? Or is it a gold toilet seat?) and being honest about it, will open you up to opportunities that you might not have noticed before.

By staying mindful about your goal and the different aspects of your life or habits that you can change to help you achieve it, you are bringing into your world, opportunities that you may not have recognized, as such, before this moment.

Another thing to be mindful about is how it feels whether it's an unexpected opportunity or part of your 'plans'. If it feels RIGHT and the follow-through for the idea seems to simply flow, then that is a clue you're on the right track.

If however it's tedious or a chore that makes you sick to think about carrying through with, you might need to sit down and go through some other ideas because it should NOT be agony.

Whatever you're doing should feel natural and good and 'in line' with the desired outcome instead of something that cuts into it at cross purposes or tries to force events into a different direction that things weren't meant to go.

So now that you have your goal, begin building the reflection of its achievement in your mind. Maybe a new house? Envision it from the entry way to the tiles in the bathroom. You don't have to do it all at once, each detail will undoubtedly have its own moment but most and more important than the details of the house it self is the *feeling* of having it. Feel the satisfaction of having achieved your dream home. Feel the love you'll be able to nurture and the memories for you, your spouse, your kids, see if you can feel the joy of your own grandchildren filling it up with love and laughter.

You've got the goal – Increased revenue

You've got the vision – The Dreamhouse

You've got the emotions – Joy, Love, bliss.

And all along you've reminded yourself of all the things in your life that you've already achieved and attained and that you're honestly grateful for, so NOW you've got the state of being that's called Gratitude.

Now, like tending a garden or keeping your yard, it's time to be mindful about how your thoughts and consequently your actions affect your ability to manifest this desire.

One of the most difficult things to do is to *act* like you have something you're working for. So, contrary to what lots of "manifestation" books will tell you, don't. You're not out to live a lie, you're out to live your truth. If you can't see yourself owning enough cars to have an elevator in your garage to get them either up or down to street level, then that's a visualization that's at cross purposes with your nature.

If, however you can envision yourself having three or four specialty cars that are well cherished, and if that visualization brings you joy instead of difficulty, then it's more likely to be in line with your nature. More is not always better. Quality over quantity may well be the mantra you find worthy of adoption.

Can you expect great things to come to you just because you want them? Of course you can, but the expectation of great things doesn't mean you don't have to put the energy of creation into it.

8. Become a Pragmatic Optimist

"The first and most important step toward success is the feeling that we CAN succeed." – Nelson Boswell.

Take the Long View

Life is a 'long haul' venture, we've been trained to "want it NOW!" and if we don't get it NOW, we throw what our parents used to call a 'kiniption fit'.

We don't like how we look? We apply make-up.

We don't like how we feel? We take a pill.

We don't like how our clothes fit? We have liposuction.

We don't like our life? We watch the Kardashians.

We're a 'quick fix' society, with everything easily within reach, the remote for life right at our fingertips and we're not above channel surfing to find something new when we don't like what we see on the t.v.

The hard and fast truth of things is that quick fixes don't work for the long haul. In order to have anything that lasts you have to prioritize. If education is what you need to get where you want to go eventually then you have to prioritize schooling. Trying to maintain the balance between schooling, partying, and socializing is hard enough when you're a college student, but when you're an adult with kids and a spouse or sick family members that you're the primary caregiver for it's not going to be any easier, but the rewards are well worth the juggling and struggling. The question you must ask yourself is "how much do I really want this?" and then it becomes a matter of acting accordingly. Like all the changes discussed here, it's not easy, but it is worth it.

Stop

Day by day we're inundated with television shows that fill our heads with notions of how 'the other half' lives. And yes we try to emulate that, especially in dialogue and mannerism, we adopt ways of dressing and speaking and eventually behaving no matter how ridiculous or detrimental to our relationships that it may be, because we see something in the character on the screen that we'd like to see in us. Whether it's the snappy come back, the glib or cutting remark meant to blow your enemy or competitor's mind, everyone wants to look, feel, and be considered witty or desirable. What most folks don't realize is that the very dialogue and possibly even actions they're trying to adopt into their own lives has been written and re-written a handful of times before the final draft gets shot. (Sorry to burst your bubble about the lovely land of television, but folks, it's NOT reality. It's a distillation of contrived circumstances. Even "Reality" TV isn't reality. The people you watch and want to emulate are little more than parodies of themselves and their worst most reprehensible qualities, this is NOT a model to try and live up to, it's a warning sign.)

We cheer when the bad guy or girl gets trounced and yet we emulate the very behaviors that brought them to their knees when the series finally runs its course, and then we wonder why *we're* so miserable? It's a literal example of 'You are who you pretend to be'. Of course on TV, the good guys are boring and people who consistently make the most positive choices lead smoother and more blissful lives. But for entertainment purposes, bliss is boring. Strife sells, sadism sells, characters who consistently make the wrong choices make us feel better about ourselves, but if that's the case then why do we adopt at least on the surface the very qualities that we abhor?

No one can be two people (except Gemini's we're born for it), of polar opposite natures and create for themselves and those around them a stable and positive life.

So the next time you're tempted to slap someone with a cutting remark or glib retort, or take part in an action whose repercussions won't dissipate with the snap of a marker or a director yelling "Cut!", do yourself a favor and stop.

Think about whether or not what you're about to say or do is going to be constructive or destructive. Peer into the future of your particular circumstances, we all have the ability to anticipate at least some of the consequences of our actions, we just need to get back in touch with that ability. How will you be perceived for what you say or do? Is that the image you want others to have of you? Is that the example you want to set for yourself or those who may look up to you that you might not even know about?

Words and actions both have vibrational frequencies that give them power on an energetic level. With that as the case, you become the one who wields the power. How will you use it? Will you use it as a bludgeon that destroys, or will you use that power to create? The choice *is* yours.

But when life's a mess, it's easier to turn on the tube and ridicule someone else and their so-called 'trials'. The problem with this escapist mentality is that it allows us to neglect our own lives so that when we're forced to actually LIVE the life we've made, we're often slammed in the face with our disappointments or the effects of our own ennui.

Try taking a media sabbatical, shut off the Facebook alert, shut off the email alert, shut off the t.v., even shut off Netflix and Youtube. Try going a weekend, 2 days, 48 hours only interacting with people face to face, (not FaceBOOK to Facebook, and not Snapchat, or Instagram....

Put the media down and back away slowly....). If they are not a being with a body in your house or your presence, don't talk with them. Leave them to their own lives for the weekend.

Since the advent of social media we have forgotten the art of being in the moment. Now I know a lot of you are probably thinking, "what's more in the moment than getting an update about my bae's status?", "what's more 'in the moment' than my best frenemy's latest selfie that makes her look 30 lbs overweight"; those may very well be, 'in the moment' moments, but when was the last time you took a series of moments to be with yourself? Can you remember the last time you spent quality time with yourself? Doing what YOU wanted to do instead of doing what you thought you should be doing based on what others were doing? When was the last time you sat in silence, no t.v., no music, no kids, no bae in the background, no pets pawing at the door? How long do you think you could last with only yourself for company? Do you even know yourself well enough to know whether or not you'd enjoy your own company?

Perhaps it's time to find out.

If spending a weekend on your own is too much of just YOU, then start with 5 minutes a day. Park in a parking lot, in the back, and just sit there, no music, phone OFF, nothing to distract you from the sound of your own breathing. Let your thoughts move through your mind, whether they circle or stream makes no difference, just let them move. Eventually they'll spend themselves and you'll find yourself sitting in silence, feeling the breath moving into and out of your body, feeling your heart beat, feeling your stomach holding itself tight, feeling your shoulders riding up so high they feel like they're trying to climb into your ears. When you notice that, let them drop, (they'll creep back up before you know it), then make them drop again.

When you've become acclimated to the feel of yourself, the weight of yourself, and the breath of yourself, you can begin to examine the truths of yourself, and begin to get to KNOW yourself. Only once you've begun to know yourself can you then begin to see what you want to change about yourself and what parts of yourself that you want to nurture and grow.

This is not an easy process. This is a worthwhile process.

9. Turn a Deaf Ear to Your Detractors.

"With great power comes great responsibility." Usually attributed to Voltaire

The greatest power you can wield is the power you hold over yourself. We must stop giving our power to others to use against us.

The Selfishness Principle

The Primary Principle of Selfishness – Allow yourself to do both what must be done as well as those great and wonderful things you aspire to do because it feels good and/or right.

Selfishness isn't necessarily what you've been raised to believe it is. Once more we've been subject to *oversimplification* of an ideal.

Most people, when contemplating the idea of selfishness imagine some kind of 'gimme' or hoarding or self-aggrandizing scenario, this isn't necessarily a true interpretation. In most cases, when the reason for the above kinds of actions are considered, at the root of those reasons is some kind of lack, and even sometimes self-loathing.

But there is a flip-side to selfishness that is more altruistic in the long run.

We've all heard, "If you don't take care of yourself first then how can you take care of someone else?"

This is usually heard more through caregiver and health care professional channels, and it's usually in reference to over-worked, over-stressed, over-taxed moms. There are some dad's who fit the bill and it applies to them as well.

It also applies to spouses caring for an ailing partner, or adult children now faced with the needs of aging and frequently ailing parents.

But it also applies to the single person, the busy friend, the activist neighbor, in short, it applies to everyone and anyone at any given time. There are times when it's necessary to go that extra mile and get something done even though it may tax our resources more than we'd like; those are the moments and the events that often help us evolve as individuals, and let's be honest, sometimes those moments also make us feel like we're being the better aspect of ourselves, and we probably are. But, when we're drained, angry, snappish, and snippy and just not feeling... right, those are the times we have to learn to recognize and weigh our own welfare against the altruistic payment we get from doing that good deed we didn't really want to, but did anyway.

It comes down to health, both physical and mental, and learning how to take those moments of quietude to get to know yourself is one of the best ways to get to know when it's time to recharge, and time just do what must be done.

Tummy Signals and Emotions

Emotions are the key to learning how to listen to our inner selves and our alignment with the universe. Your emotions are the first biofeedback mechanism we have that tells us whether we're doing something right or something wrong. Whether what we're doing is something good for us or bad for us, physically, emotionally, spiritually, our BODY sends us signals. That squirrelly feeling in the tummy? That loose heavy feeling in the bowels, the cold clammy feelings are typical physiological responses to some kind of anticipated negative impact on a person's systems.

As a child I'd heard people saying, 'listen to your guts', 'your guts'll tell you what's right or wrong', but no one ever told me HOW to listen to them. So I moved through daily life thinking that my instincts didn't really give a damn about daily life, and like a typical little sister, I pushed and pushed until I got a belly response. Of course usually by the time my belly did say something about what I was doing, to tell me it was wrong, I was already in trouble.

So even though to a lot of folks it's kind of a 'duh'! Here it is. When your belly isn't saying much of anything, you're more than likely on the right track. Now if you're on that right track and you make a decision that suddenly has your tummy doing BAD kinds of acrobatics (the cold clammy, nauseating in a bad way kind), remember you do have the option of changing your mind. As long as you haven't followed through on the decision yet, you can STOP and change direction which will bring your tummy back to a neutral state of non-reactivity.

Of course then again we all come to those moments where our tummies are going crazy because of something positive. Positive excitement can make you feel nauseous but you probably won't mind it whereas negative emotion nausea will make you want to crawl into a hole and not come out.

The occasionally confusing thing about the body's signals is that for something positive or negative the physiologic response might be nearly identical, which is why we have emotions to further guide our decision making process. Use the happiness, joyful anticipation, the color of the emotion that accompanies the body signals if you're not sure what you're planning is the right thing or not.

Think in terms of a marriage proposal. Guys, you've found the woman of your dreams, you're absolutely certain she's the one you want to wake up with for the rest of your life and in spite of the fact that your belly is dancing like a leprechaun that just got his gold back, the image that comes to you, that you just can't wait for, is that warm glowy far away day when you're both old and wrinkly and couldn't be happier for the decades together.

Of course, if your first reaction to the idea of marrying her (ladies this is applicable to you too!) is kind of colorless and cold like the bottom of the Mariana Trench and you can't see anything but lead weights around your ankles, you might want to reconsider. Men actually understand the difference better than women do in a lot of cases, thoughtful men (I'm talking about the kind of thoughtful that weighs implications against as many aspects of their lives as possible), will also pay attention to how the woman of their choice makes THEM FEEL. Women often have a tendency, (STILL), to put aside how a man makes them feel, especially when contemplating his ability to provide for offspring. Fortunately in today's world we can begin to consider partnering with someone for real love and fulfillment rather than out of desperation, fear, or social pressure.

> Fear of being alone is the biggest reason for marrying someone against your body's wishes. There's a reason why

experts propone that it's best to date for at least a year before getting married. Give the Oxytocin a chance to die down so you can see each other without rose colored glasses on. Strip away the idea that either of you is going to change the other (cause that ain't gonna happen), and see if those warts are something you can live with. If he or she has a habit that makes you want to scream a month into the dating, then the lifetime is not going to work.

On the subject of marriage a lot of people also make the mistake of marrying because they feel obligated to, either to the other person, or because of some societal expectation. Again, the fact is, if you haven't married that person yet there's probably a reason. Do both of you the honor and respect of deep consideration before folding to outside pressure. *See Ch 8.

So while this is just an example, it's a pertinent one since marriage is a HUGE change. It's another opportunity to listen to your body (your belly, not that wonderful land of blissful sensation between your legs), and your emotions and make the best choice possible for all parties concerned. Marrying out of fear of being alone or because of societal, family, or peer pressure will rarely if ever merit positive results for the future, (ie, offspring).

The above is just one way to use the pairing of emotion with physiologic response to achieve the most fulfilling possible outcome. The HABIT of separating our emotions from our 'chosen' course of action, in the name of "Productivity" or "the Almighty Dollar" has become a quality employers seek. But in this moment look at the fate of the employers who espouse such 'ectomy' of self as a virtue. They are failing and falling.

This isn't to say that if your passion is Law, that you have to give it up in order to bring yourself into alignment with YOUR Universal harmony. Maybe it just means that you need to consider a change from being a prosecutor to a defense lawyer, or vice versa. There are options and ways and means to feed your passions and allow them to feed your LIFE while staying true to both who ARE and who you will to BECOME.

In order to pass forward a legacy of true choice, you must first make your own. The moment is mutable.

Who you are today is a stepping stone to who you will be tomorrow. Fulfillment doesn't always mean riches, or status, or being the one the Jones' have to keep up with. Fulfillment is only one element that comprises the ability to look in your own eyes in the mirror in the morning or at night and KNOW you held true to what you KNOW is right inside. It's part of the ability to sleep soundly knowing you did the best you could today. It's part of the ability to enjoy a meal with your family and go to your kid's soccer match without worrying if the coach is an ass or an asset, or if your kid is going to be scarred for life because he or she got benched. It's knowing that when you get home from the game you can say to your child, "You did GREAT today." And mean it because *today* they did as great as they could, and you understand that.

It's also the ability to assure those kids of yours that tomorrow will bring them more opportunities to see what they can do better, or HOW they can do it better.

This is where the brightest part of you really gets to shine into the future. Embrace it, love it, and when necessary cry because holding those boundaries for those kids can sometimes hurt more than you can imagine. But the only thing you absolutely MUST do, is never let them forget that you LOVE them, and sometimes love means saying "No.".

So the point is, use your emotions as a barometer, that's what they're there for.

10. Let Others Bear Their Own Baggage – You Have Enough to Carry.

We all know people who just love to spew their misfortune into the air around everyone they can. We know people who love to deflate your day because, as we also know, 'misery loves company'. Some of them are friends, some are family members, others are co-workers and some are simply grumpy people we may meet on the street or in the grocery store or ... anywhere.

These are the people that have a tendency to perpetuate their own misery by not making changes to their own lives, and as their misery compounds with inaction over inaction, they love to engage you, in carrying some of their burden.

They lay their troubles on you as if you're a pack mule, then seem to either wind up flitting about like butterflies in a breeze (once they've unloaded on you), or they continue to drag everyone around them down.

We've called them 'energy vampires' in the past. You know who they are, they're the ones that suck the life and joy out of a room faster than Homer Simpson can scarf down a donut. And whenever they call to say, 'let's go out', or, 'c'mon over', your heart skips a beat and your tummy starts to squirm an unmistakable message that warns, "Dooooon't do it!" And yet we do.

It's a horribly difficult thing to tell a friend that you don't want to hear their problems, but I'm not talking about the kind of 'venting' that most friends do when they first get together. You sit down, you talk about what's bugging you, hash it out, then once the emotional charge has worn off, you laugh about it and move on to subjects that make you happy. That's normal.

If it tends more often to be that you sit down, and your friend starts venting, and won't let you get a word in edgewise; and it's about the same thing over and over again ad infinitum, but their behavior about the situation doesn't change, *that* is when they're putting their troubles on you and letting you carry them.

These are the kind of people who brush off what's going on in *your* life when *you* need to vent, and turn the conversation back to themselves and their own troubles. No matter how serious or silly your problem may be they don't simply give what's bothering you any credence or weight.

Sadly, this is an indicator of how much or how little they respect YOU.

Everyone needs to talk out their troubles once in a while, and that's one of the things that friends are for, whether it be your life partner, or just someone you meet for lunch a few times a year and chat with. You spend time with that person presumably because you enjoy their company, and hopefully they enjoy yours, but sometimes their actions prove that they're more interested in you as a verbal whipping post than as an equal. That is when it's time to advise them about your feelings.

Having to tell someone that you feel as if they don't care about your problems, that you feel as if they only want to hang out when they have something they need to get off their chest, and that makes you feel as if they don't care for you as much as you care for them, is beyond difficult. Your friend will, most likely at first, be defensive, then get angry, and possibly even storm out. If you can accept any of those actions, then you can feel confident in talking with them about your feelings. One of the hardest things to do is to keep the conversation from being confrontational and accusatory.

Friends, lovers, and even family members have been lost because of conversations gone awry.

Part of the problem, which has already been touched on earlier in chapter 9, and even so far back as chapters 1 and 2, is that the people in your life have their own scripts, their own programs that they are impelled and sometimes compelled to adhere to.

In other words, they just can't help themselves! And they really can't! The only person who can tell you that you're ready for change is yourself, and if your friends or family members, or co-workers, or whoever your personal energy vampire is; can't or won't respect your feelings, then sometimes it's better to take some time away.

With friends, you may find it easier than you think to walk away and let them live their own lives while you move forward with yours. The fact is that when a friendship has reached its end, walking away from it can be like stepping out of a pair of old, worn out flip flops.

Before the previous paragraph is read as an encouragement to use people and toss them away once they no longer serve you or your purpose, it's not. Friendships come and go, they have their time and that time has to be recognized as something special and necessary; but we do outgrow, or simply move in different directions after a while, and that's not a bad thing at all. It just means that you were where you needed to be, and so was that other person.

Co-workers are a different story, most often it's easier to simply pull back little by little without having to address the situation, that is, of course, as long as the situation isn't something that drives you stark raving mad or has jeopardized your standing among your superiors or peers.

Family tends to be where it gets toughest. There are a couple different schools of thought on the subject; one being that "they're your family so they have to keep loving you no matter what", and the other being "they're family, so they'll never change so why should I bother?" There is a third option that everyone fears at some point or another and that is, "they'll kick me out/disown me." Although that third one is rare, it does happen, and it's up to the individual to decide whether or not it's an outcome that's worth the risk.

The thing about family though is that it's easier to understand a family member's position on something, because you know their history, and therefore their programming.

For example, if your parents were raised deeply, religious, and because of that they forced you to go to a religious school, and now they want you to go to a religious University or they won't pay for your continuing education, then it's up to you to decide which sacrifice you'll make if they absolutely refuse to discuss any other option.

Most of the time people, even parents will come around if presented with sound information (I don't like to use the word arguments, because you're trying NOT to argue, you're trying to logically and rationally provide information to support your stance. Arguments tend to come along anyway, so I'd rather not encourage them here.). And if after you've made your case, they still cannot deviate from their own programming, then it's up to you to accept that they're not in a position to change at that time.

Hopefully, the love will always be there so that as time does go by, and you live the sound, ethical, moral, upstanding life that you choose, those around you will be able to see that the changes and growth you've attained have only made you someone they're more proud to have around.

Basic Tools

Some of the most basic tools that are available to help bring about the destiny you choose have been taught and advocated for years if not centuries.

The first is probably the longest lived tool among humans, and that is meditation.

Wikipedia defines meditation as: "Meditation is a practice where an individual trains the mind or induces a mode of consciousness, either to realize some benefit or for the mind to simply acknowledge its content without becoming identified with that content, or as an end in itself.

The term meditation refers to a broad variety of practices that includes techniques designed to promote relaxation, build internal energy or life force (qi, ki, prana, etc.) and develop compassion, love, patience, generosity, and forgiveness."

And continues with: "The word meditation carries different meanings in different contexts. Meditation has been practiced since antiquity as a component of numerous religious traditions and beliefs. Meditation often involves an internal effort to self-regulate the mind in some way. Meditation is often used to clear the mind and ease many health concerns, such as high blood pressure, depression, and anxiety. It may be done sitting, or in an active way—for instance, Buddhist monks involve awareness in their day-to-day activities as a form of mind-training. Prayer beads or other ritual objects are commonly used during meditation in order to keep track of or remind the practitioner about some aspect of that training."

There are a myriad variety of meditative practices as well as reasons to meditate as you can see from the above quote.

Another technique that's been touched on, however fleetingly, is creative visualization. The ability to see yourself doing things that represent the changes you want to make in your life.

The subconscious mind works in symbols, not words. That's why you can show anyone on the planet (except perhaps for certain tribes that refuse contact with outsiders), a drawing of a toilet and they'll get the idea what you're talking about.

Our subconscious mind understood symbols, colors, textures, tastes and smells long before our brains were made to understand words. So it only makes sense that coupling meditative practices with symbolism of YOUR idea of success, power, wealth, security, or love would make these things more attainable to you.

Synesthesia

Synesthesia, (sin-es-thee-sh-uh) is a condition in which an individual may see the number 5, but see it in the color green, and maybe even sometimes while smelling oranges. It's a sort of cross-wiring of the input devices.

I believe that in some ways we are all synesthetes. We all have had experiences in which the scent of something will trigger a memory, sometimes with full sound or vision or both.

Take a moment to write down what you experience when you think of baking chocolate chip cookies. Or your mother's perfume.

Write what you smell, any underlying scents that come along in a secondary way. Write sounds that come with the memory of the scent, and even go so far as to try to remember any physical sensations, like the warm gooeyness of a hot cooking falling apart in your hand.

If you can't think of anything or aren't stimulated by the idea of foods, then think of a moment of warmth and comfort, softness and try to remember the scent that comes along with it, and most importantly remember how you felt INSIDE.

Another method you can use is something like the "Vision Board" that was touted in The Secret.

Just as we put up pictures of skinny people on the fridge when we're dieting, or muscular people or both to help remind us of what we want for ourselves, the idea of the vision board is simply to help us keep our goals in mind. It's actually up to the individual to make those things happen by TAKING ACTION.

Another part of using pictures of a person who isn't yourself is that IT ISN'T YOU. The house you put on your vision board isn't yours, it's not necessarily YOUR vision, it's someone else's. Therein lies the problem. The best visualizations you can obtain are those that come from within.

If you can't visualize yourself thin or muscular, then imagine the FEELING of it. Are you light on your feet? Can you bend over to tie your shoes (assuming some people still do that), without feeling like you have to hold your breath to do so? Can you imagine striding through your house in your underwear and not feeling things jiggle that aren't supposed to?

Can you feel yourself carrying your grocery bags as though they were no more than the weight of a blanket? Can you imagine maneuvering with grace and stamina through a crowd of people or just through your day? Can you imagine wearing a t-shirt that fits snugly across your body and accentuates your muscles instead of your... not muscles?

Whatever your goal is, if you have to start by using pictures of someone else or their idea of wealth and security, to start the ball rolling before you learn to visualize these things for yourself, or whether you can make these images on your own from the get-go, the important thing is to use this technique in conjunction with meditation. These two methods together will provide you with the most powerful internal motivation that you can experience.

Another method that can help you is the Kappas Mental Bank method.

This method uses the ideomotor skill of cursive writing, combined with a 'mental monetary reward' that activates rudimentary math skills (all you need to be able to do is the basic four – add, subtract, multiply, and divide) which further helps you embed your goals and strategies into your subconscious mind, making success all that more readily attainable, that much more quickly.

Utilizing all of these techniques will help you stay focused on your vision, and help you clarify the end results you want while keeping your mind on working out how to overcome the obstacles that are anticipated as well as those that will inevitably pop into existence.

Why Failure Really Happens

Development coach and entrepreneur John Assaraf (The Secret, Praxis Neuroscience), has a really neat way of explaining why failure really happens. His model is the exact result of those indoctrinations I talked about in chapter 6.

Your concept of who you are must be in line with the goals you want to achieve. If you can see yourself having, doing, and being your ideal, then you can achieve it BUT first you must control the demons of your indoctrination. You MUST tame those voices that tell you you're not good enough, or too fat, or too ugly, or don't deserve success.

If you can't control those ideas that were placed in your head by others, ("Who do you think you are? You don't have what it takes!") then you will never be able to move out of the status quo, which is exactly where your subconscious believes you should be, because it constantly hears the rhetoric of your indoctrination.

You have been brainwashed by others to continue brainwashing yourself so that you will always be exactly who and what SOMEONE ELSE WANTS you to be!

One of the reasons the vast majority of 'self-help' devices, services, and advocates espouse meditation and visualization to help you achieve your goals, is because it works.

Initially it may be difficult to see yourself moving into a 50,000 square foot mansion, or running a corporation, but through meditation and visualization techniques you can build, at your own pace, a vision of that life that fits with the obtaining of the small, attainable goals you've set up from chapter 4.

These meditative and visualization exercises help change the way you perceive yourself and what you're worthy of.

When I was a teenager, my stepdad told me that Yoga was a tool of Satan and that if I did it, I would go to hell. (There were a lot of things he told me I was going to go to hell for). He claimed that because it induced an altered state of mind, that it allowed Satan to come into your consciousness and that by voluntarily altering your state of mind you were welcoming possession. (Never mind the fact that sleep, alcohol, music, dance and many other activities [and a few substances] are also mind altering and yet not commonly considered avenues for possession by Satan.)

I scoffed, and being the precocious child I was, told him I'd save him a seat on the way down.

It wasn't until later though that I made the connection between his own indoctrination about religion, self-loathing, and fear of change that I began to understand why he could've said what he did. No matter which way I looked at it, the end reason was fear of one kind or another.

Fear of change is something we all have to deal with at some point in time or another, simply because changing leads to something that is largely unknown or uncertain.

Keep in mind though, that if you have your plan, and if you are taking those small steps toward reaching your goal, you are building certainty. You are building a path to a certain destination from which you will begin building another path to another destination. And once you know where you're going, and how you plan to get there, the uncertainty factor no longer exists. You are creating a new KNOWN aspect to your life. Fear can no longer hold sway over you.

EPILOGUE

"Life is choice." – Anonymous

It's human nature to seek personal fulfillment, it's because of this desire that the world is full of 'self-help' guru's and systems, many of which have helped many people, but none of which have worked for everyone who has tried them.

Almost every single one of them give the same advice, what differs are the methods of obtaining the 'promised' results.

One of the reasons there are so many methods is because the ways in which we learn are as myriad and varied as are people. How we connect with information goes hand in hand with how readily that information is absorbed and whether or not it's applied.

My name is JA Carlton, I'm a 27 year veteran of the Health Care field. I started out in the 90's as a Massage Therapist, then in the 2000's became a Radiologic Technologist. In 2014 I became a hypnotherapist, and am now an LMRT (Limited Medical Radiologic Technician) Instructor in Austin Texas. Since my early teens I've been practicing ways of exerting autonomy, and creating a life of satisfaction and fulfillment free of the judgments and expectations of others.

The information contained here has been compiled and personally tested over a lifetime. Any health advice is not intended to supplant or replace information and the input of your medical provider. Any emotional, intellectual or psychological insights are not intended to supplant or replace interactions with whatever advisors you choose.

Don't miss out!

Visit the website below and you can sign up to receive emails whenever JA Carlton publishes a new book. There's no charge and no obligation.

https://books2read.com/r/B-A-SJFZ-NVALC

BOOKS 2 READ

Connecting independent readers to independent writers.